Christmas Thoughts About Love

Also by Donald E. Saunders, Jr., M.D.

To Improve the Health of the People:
An insider's view of the campaign for the
University of South Carolina School of Medicine (2005)

Christmas Thoughts About Love

A CARDIOLOGIST SPEAKS FROM HIS HEART

Donald E. Saunders, Jr. M.D.

ISBN:	Hardcover	978-1-4257-5710-6
	Softcover	978-1-4257-5708-3

This book was printed in the United States of America.

To order additional copies of this book, contact:
Xlibris Corporation
1-888-795-4274
www.Xlibris.com
Orders@Xlibris.com

38944

Contents

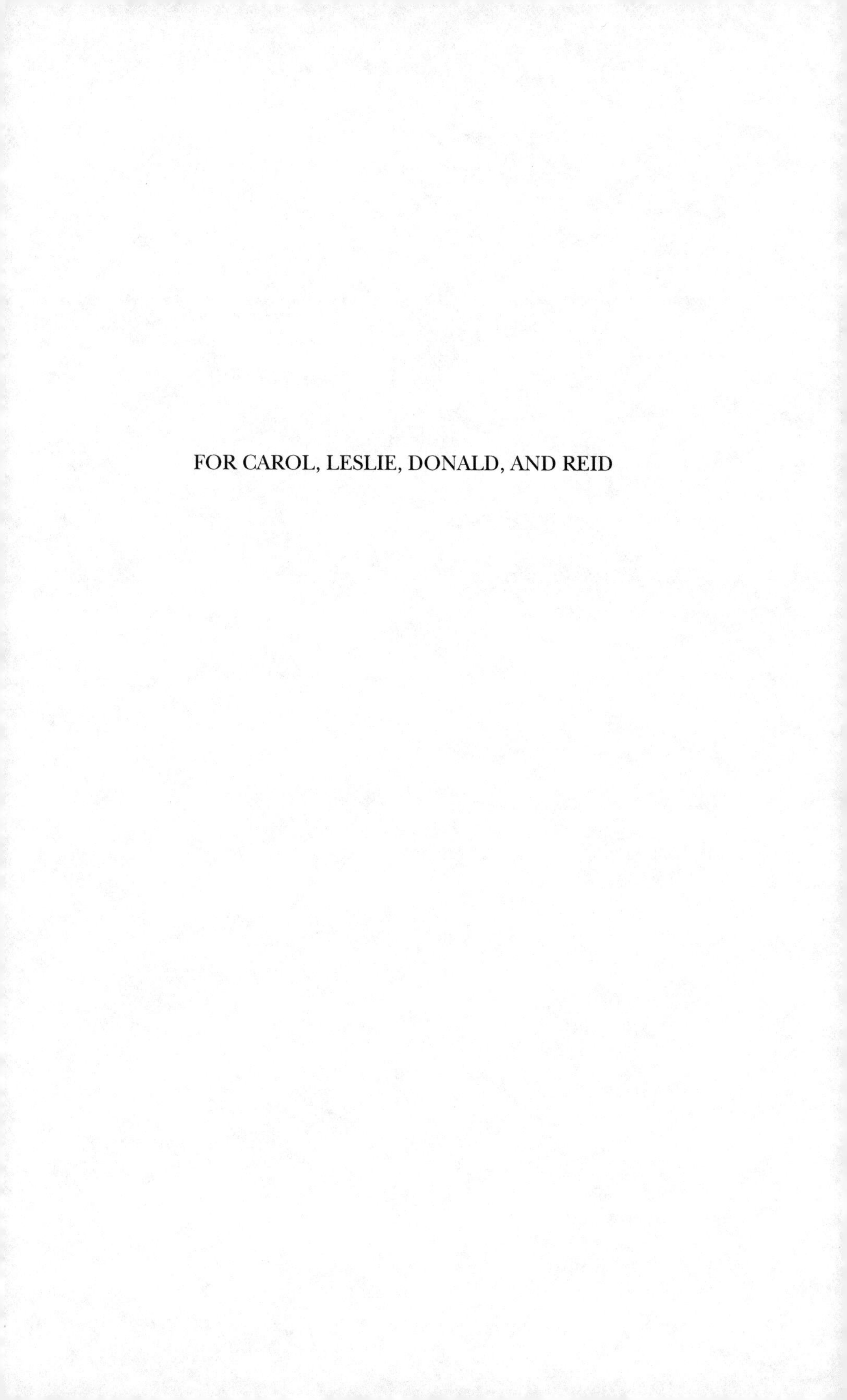

FOR CAROL, LESLIE, DONALD, AND REID

Acknowledgments

THE KOSMOS CLUB OF COLUMBIA, SOUTH CAROLINA, provided both a setting and an inspiration for these essays. Each was first presented as a "five-minute paper" to the club. Established in 1904, Kosmos is composed in equal parts of town (with purposely diverse occupations) and gown (University of South Carolina faculty) members. At monthly meetings, in a setting of good food and drink and lively conversation, each member in rotation reads an original paper, usually lasting forty to fifty minutes, followed by questions and comments. Because of the time pressures of Christmas, the December meeting is devoted to six to ten five-minute papers. For the past fifteen years one of the December papers has been my essay about love.

Thank you, Barbara Brannon, for encouragement and editing of the early essays and to Stephen G. Hoffius for editing the final product. Paul Rossmann produced the cover design and the Love Vector illustration, which was originally contributed by Dee McFarland. The family picture was by Reid Saunders. Thanks to Theodore J. Hopkins, Jr., for calling my attention to the Helen Keller quote and to Mimi Ackerman for her expert proofreading.

Introduction and Prescription

The best and most beautiful things in the world
cannot be
seen or even touched.
They must be felt within the heart.
—Helen Keller
blind and deaf educator

WE KNOW WHEN THE CHRISTMAS SEASON IS HERE: shorter days, colder nights, frenetic retail trade. Social events multiply, lights adorn trees on Main Street, *The Nutcracker* is performed, Christmas background music blares everywhere, and sleep deprivation accumulates. Free time is less available to step back and reflect on the real meaning of Christmas: a Christian religious celebration of the birth of Jesus Christ, the champion of love and peace. Meanwhile, the news media continue to report the opposite: hate and war.

In December 1990 I responded to a personal need to alter this situation by assigning myself some homework: produce a short essay, one which could be read in about five minutes, on the subject of Christmas and love. The result was the first essay in this book, which was well received by family and friends. Clearly it was not a typical "Christmas letter." The exercise was repeated in December 1991 with similar results, initiating a "fifteen-game hitting streak"—an annual essay each December through 2004. Some essays are philosophical, some meditative, others are deeply personal.

Love is a one-syllable, commonly used noun and verb which is packed with complexity and power. Not surprisingly, almost all authors of "great books" have written about love. I cannot imagine a time when the "last word" about love is written. My subject is the love of true friendship, of parent for child, and brotherly love—not erotic, sexual love. My theme is the need for more love informing our individual and collective lives. It's a polemic for love rather than a discussion of whether love is a universal good.

These essays are located in both horizontal and vertical time. Calendar time always moves horizontally. The essays were written and presented twelve months apart, during the Christmas seasons in 1990 through 2004. Sometimes contemporary events are mentioned which may establish the horizontal time when they were written. Yet both love and the Christmas story are unchanging through the years, placing them in vertical time, when time stands still, because our attention is fully captured and we are oblivious to horizontal time.

Christmas is both a religious and a secular holiday, celebrated by a pause in our routine—at least a day or two off work. It presents an opportunity to step back and reflect. Regardless of one's religious beliefs or lack thereof, love is an accessible value. The problem is that love must compete with all the other distractions of daily life. Christmas can serve as both a reminder and an opportunity to reflect on love—its meaning, its effect on our relationships, its power and mystery.

I suggest that each essay first be read through at normal reading speed and then read again with pauses at points where understanding is missing or disagreements surface. Although there are references to contemporary events, each essay is self-contained and doesn't require reading in a particular order. Each is intended to be a starting point for further reflection and, I hope, discussion, rather than an evidence-based answer to life's most important questions.

My annual pauses during the Christmas season to think about love have had a positive effect on my life at the most basic level—my soul, if you will. Since I share my basic nature with all other humans, I have no reservation about prescribing the practice for you. (Doctors do write prescriptions, you know.) Even though the Food and Drug Administration has had nothing to say about love, I am certain that pausing to reflect on love and writing down your thoughts is safe, effective, and will not cause allergic reactions. If you like it, this prescription has unlimited refills and will remain free of charge.

This collection is a gift to you, the reader. If you try it yourself, I guarantee your attention will be focused, for a while at least, on a subject important to the human spirit. If you wish to share your thoughts with me, my e-mail address is dsaunder@richmed.medpark.sc.edu.

December 1990

Love Vectors

ONCE AGAIN WE CELEBRATE THE BIRTH AND LIFE OF one of the great teachers from the past. By word and deed the message of Jesus of Nazareth was love and its corollary, peace. Meanwhile, we are once again mobilizing for war, this time in the Persian Gulf. Why, after two thousand years, haven't we learned the great teacher's lesson?

In Pat Conroy's novel *The Prince of Tides,* protagonist Tom Wingo tells his sister's psychiatrist, "There's only one thing difficult about being a man, Doctor. Only one thing. They don't teach us how to love. It's a secret they keep from us."

Poet Robert Bly, in a Bill Moyers television program called "A Gathering of Men," observed: "But, you know, men are not *hiding* their feelings from women. Men look down inside and they don't see . . . anything in there. There's a feeling of numbness that, for men, comes early in life."

In American culture, love is ritualized in religious services and trivialized in popular music, but rarely is it contemplated with serious intent. Among some, love has even become a liability, a negative attribute, as expressed in the best-selling book, *Women Who Love Too Much.*

And yet we all know, don't we, that love is incomparable, transcending, uncompromised by space and time, multidimensional, extraordinarily powerful, and a necessary ingredient for a happy human life.

I've begun to think of love in terms of vectors. In the physics of forces, the vector symbol is an arrow whose point indicates a direction in space and whose length represents a magnitude of force. In the basic unit of two persons in a truly loving relationship, there must be four love vectors of about equal magnitude, each of which points in a different direction.

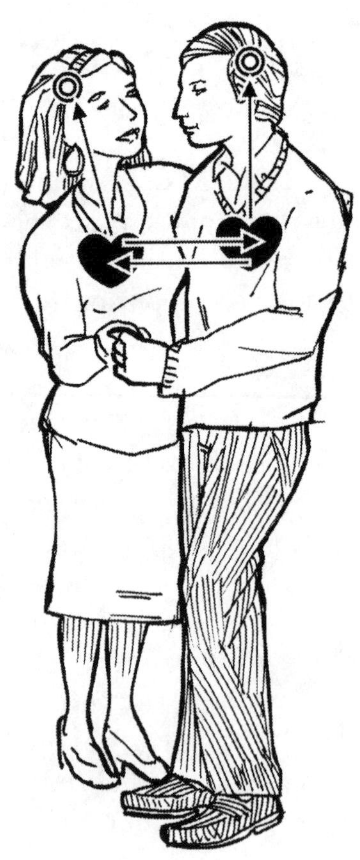

Most of us would intuitively agree on the two reciprocating vectors pointing in parallel from each person to the other, like Cupid's arrows.

Perhaps less obvious is the fact that the other two love vectors must point inward to the individual soul or spirit of each person, indicating the necessity of a love for *self* that is at least equal in magnitude to love for *another*. The importance of self-love is a concept at least as old as the ancient civilizations of West and East and as new as contemporary psychological theory and practice.

Aristotle, in the *Nicomachean Ethics,* debated the question, "[W]hether a man should love himself most, or someone else." The great philosopher concluded that "the good man should be a lover of self for he will both himself profit by doing noble acts, and will benefit his fellows, but the wicked man should not; for he will hurt both himself and his neighbors, following as he does evil passions."

In the ancient East, the practice of yoga arose from early Hindu religion and the culture of the Indian subcontinent. Yoga seeks spirituality, or God, within each person, with the accompanying love for the God within.

Love also provides a theme for contemporary thought—consider psychiatrist M. Scott Peck's bestseller *The Road Less Traveled.* Peck defines love as "the will to extend one's self for the purpose of nurturing one's own or another's spiritual growth."

Thus there is remarkable agreement, across the ages, that we can only love others to the extent that we love ourselves. Relationships routinely founder when we depend on the object of our love to fill what we consciously or, more commonly, unconsciously perceive as an unloved blemish or void within us. A loving relationship is not a dependent relationship. Love seeks to give rather than to get, or to get only by giving. While one wishes to be loved in return, demands must be few and not necessary to meet one's own unmet needs.

Could it be that this nation of ours looks inward and doesn't love itself because of what it sees? Could that lead to repeated hostile actions against one external enemy after another? I don't know, but I do wonder and worry about it.

These thoughts about love in the Christmas season are my gift of friendship. I invite you to join me in thinking about love. Pick a quiet time, when you are alone, and contemplate love in your life. Then surprise your family and friends by actually speaking about it. If you're like me, this will be hard to do. But if you do, I predict that some primal force will stir within your deepest parts, and you will take a step towards actualizing your very own life.

December 1991

Lovers and Warriors

WHAT A DIFFERENCE A YEAR MAKES! A YEAR AGO, WHEN I composed my first "Christmas Thoughts about Love" our nation was mobilizing for the war that was fought shortly thereafter in the same part of the world where Jesus lived two thousand years ago. As the holiday celebrating the birth of Jesus approaches in 1991, our President and his envoys have been active brokers in seeking Middle Eastern peace by promoting the first direct negotiations between Israel and neighboring Arab states.

Jungian psychologists might conclude that our political leaders are now more controlled by the archetype of the Lover; whereas, last year the Warrior was in control. The great Swiss psychologist and psychiatrist Carl G. Jung found that at the level of the deep unconscious the human psyche is grounded in certain patterns and energy configurations that provide foundations for human behavior. Jung termed these "archetypes," the primordial images we all possess.

In their recent book *King Warrior Magician Lover,* Robert Moore and Douglas Gillette describe four of these archetypes in modern terms readily accessible to lay readers. The Lover, they claim, feels sensitive to his environment and connected to the world in all its splendor and wonder. His doors and windows are open; his walls are down; his sensory powers are turned on and tuned in. He feels compassionately and empathetically connected to others. He wants to touch and be touched, both physically and emotionally.

Lover energy is the source of spirituality. Spirituality requires relationships and connectedness—such as a feeling of oneness with fellow human beings, with nature, or with God.

The Lover ignores boundaries, making himself available to give and receive, but at the same time making himself vulnerable to both the joy and the pain that love brings. To counteract the danger of openness, love is the source of a hot, powerful energy that fuels the courage to persist despite pain and vulnerability. As the apostle Paul wrote in I Corinthians, *charity*—meaning love of humanity—"beareth all things," "endureth all things," and "never faileth." Among faith, hope, and charity, charity ranks number one.

Lover energy seeks understanding of others, togetherness, and peace; whereas the Warrior feels indifference towards others, maintains boundaries of separation, and prepares for war. The construction of the Berlin Wall was a Warrior-based act; the dismantling of the Wall was driven by Lover energy.

There are obviously times when we as individuals or as a nation must appropriately employ our Warrior energy. However, during my lifetime I have seen the Warrior too frequently dominate our collective behavior.

Why not take some time this Christmas season to get in better touch with the Lover archetype within each of us? After all, it does seem reasonable to honor the birth of Jesus by recalling his simple but still revolutionary message: God overwhelmingly loves humankind, and humanity needs to receive this love and let it flow outward to others.

One doesn't even need to believe in Jesus or God to follow this process, since the Lover is part of your human psyche and mine. One suggestion that I have found helpful is to answer the question: "What draws me into life?" If your answer is at least in part love for one or more others, let that be the opening to explore further what love means to you as you go about your daily life. Then share your thoughts with someone else. I predict that sharing will be a much-appreciated Christmas gift to yourself and to your family and friends.

December 1992

God and Love

WITH THE PASSAGE OF ANOTHER YEAR, WE SEE FURTHER movement of our national purpose toward love. This time last year I commented that our President had moved from preparing for war to working actively for peace in the Middle East. This year he has decided to employ our military forces to help feed and save the people of Somalia—with no apparent selfish motivation. Since we, the people of the United States, are sovereign, our President acts for us. Love is indeed mysterious and powerful and appears to be gaining some ascendancy in our collective personality.

In this age of unprecedented scientific knowledge of nature—everything from human nature to astronomy—dare we suppose that a supreme being might be somehow infusing love among leaders of powerful nations? Great thinkers warn us that God is a very difficult subject to discuss outside of a community of faith. Two learned and thoughtful twentieth-century writers and thinkers whom I admire are Mortimer J. Adler and Carl

G. Jung. Adler is an American philosopher with whom I have studied. He originated the *Great Books of the Western World* series and chairs the board of editors of the *Encyclopedia Britannica.* Jung was a Swiss psychiatrist and depth psychologist who broke away from Sigmund Freud and gained a great following for his own psychoanalytic theories and methods.

In his book *How to Think about God,* published in 1980 when he was seventy-seven years old, Adler used philosophical methods to characterize God as a supreme being who is the creator and preserver of the cosmos. He does not claim to have philosophical proof that God is also a being with loving moral goodness and an intervening presence in earthly matters. The latter is a matter of faith.

What Adler does do is make it painfully clear that the challenge is great to prove that God exists by philosophy, without depending on faith. Adler knows that the philosophic method of thinking about God requires commonly understood definitions of attributes, without which argument is impossible. He uses five positive descriptors of God: an existing, necessary being, a living being, an all-knowing being (omniscience), and a willing being having the power to enact what is willed (omnipotence).

But those positive, or affirmative, attributes must be used analogically and not literally, making it necessary to qualify every positive descriptor by adding to or modifying the descriptor with all or part of the following cluster of negative notes: immaterial, incorporeal; non-temporal, eternal; imperceptible; infinite; independent; unconditioned; and uncaused by another.

The reason for this complexity in terminology is the simple fact that man and God are radically different in kind. We can only know human life, not God's divine life. This fact explains why fundamentalists who worship literal reading of a version of the Bible, rather than symbolic reading, are impious and wrong.

I participated in an Adler-led seminar on God in which he illustrated, slapping the table for emphasis, literal compared to symbolic reading of the Bible by saying Jesus couldn't sit at the right hand of God because "God has no right hand."

Often at the end of a seminar the participants expressed their appreciation of Adler by a skit poking fun at our master teacher—which he very much enjoyed. I pretended to be a camper at "Captain Mortimer's Camp," writing a letter to my parents telling them what I learned. "I learned today that God is all powerful and has no right hand. I figure He must have a heck of a left jab!"

On the other hand, Jung, near the end of his autobiography *Memories, Dreams, and Reflections,* reflects on love and God from his discipline and perspective. In this book, written when he was past eighty and published after his death in 1961, Jung writes,

"I sometimes feel that Paul's words—'Though I speak with the tongues of men and of angels, and have not love'—might well be the first condition of all cognition and the quintessence of divinity itself. Whatever the learned interpretation may be of the sentence 'God is love,' the words affirm the *complexio oppositorum* of the Godhead. In my medical experience as well as in my own life I have again and again been faced with the mystery of love, and have never been able to explain what it is . . . . Man can try to name love, showering upon it all the names at his command, and still he will involve himself in endless self-deceptions. If he possesses a grain of wisdom, he will lay down his arms and name the unknown by the more unknown . . . that is, by the name of God."

Admittedly, Adler and Jung are taking different approaches to their subjects. But I believe the experiences of these two prolific scholars are complementary. Both emphasize the complexity, the conceptual problems, the inadequacy of language, the power, the mystery, and the importance of attempting to understand God and love in our time. However, with proper humility, I suggest that simply repeating words from an age long past will not do for either subject if we are looking for help, as I am, in finding answers to those enduring questions: What is the meaning, if any, of life? How should I live my life? Writings of Mortimer Adler and Carl Jung have helped me find some, certainly not all, of my own answers. Both Adler and Jung left behind extensive writings for those who seek the answers.

December 1993

Divine Love

PERHAPS THE MOST DIFFICULT OF THE VARIOUS FORMS of love to experience fully and truly is divine love. By divine love I mean an unconditional love of the universe, especially the human component that encompasses ourselves, our neighbors, and even our enemies. The ancient Greek word for love of this type was *agape*. The Latin word was *caritas*.

From *caritas* we derive our English word "charity." Although another meaning of the word is "alms for the poor and needy," in the New Testament charity is listed among the Christian virtues of faith, hope, and charity. There, as the greatest of the virtues, it means divine love or love of God.

The expression "charity begins at home" comes from a passage written by Sir Thomas Browne in the seventeenth century: "But how shall we expect charity towards others, when we are uncharitable to ourselves? Charity begins at home, is the voice of the world; yet is every man his own greatest enemy, and, as it were, his own executioner."

The concept of charity clearly denies the validity of love restricted to one's own kind, whether it be self, family, society, nation, race, ethnic group, or religion. Charity has no boundaries, extending instead to all. It may well be true that love restricted to one's kin, tribe or close neighbors is at least in part a Darwinian genetic trait which helps to ensure survival. Experience demonstrates that commandments to love strangers—those of different ethnic groups and even one's enemies—challenge our ability to do so. It just doesn't seem "natural."

Yet in Matthew 5:44-46 Jesus says explicitly, "But I tell you this: Love your enemies and pray for your persecutors; only so you can be children of your heavenly Father, who causes the sun to rise on good and bad alike, and sends rain on the innocent and the wicked. If you love only those who love you, what reward can you expect?"

How to act out difficult moral virtues such as charity probably is best taught by stories which engage our imaginations. For instance, consider the special value of this Jewish parable:

There was once a rabbi in a small Jewish village in Russia who vanished every Friday for several hours. The devoted villagers boasted that during these hours their rabbi ascended to heaven to talk with God. A skeptical newcomer arrived in town, determined to discover where the rabbi really was.

One Friday morning the newcomer hid near the rabbi's house, watched him rise, say his prayers, and put on the clothes of a peasant. He saw him take an ax and go into the forest, chop down a tree, and gather a large bundle of wood.

Next the rabbi proceeded to a shack in the poorest section of the village in which lived an old woman. He left her the wood, which was enough for the week. The rabbi then quietly returned to his own house.

The story concludes that the newcomer stayed on in the village and became a disciple of the rabbi. And whenever he hears one of his fellow villagers say, "On Friday morning our rabbi ascends all the way to heaven," the newcomer quietly adds, "If not higher."

December 1994

Soul Love

ONE OF THE MOST INSIGHTFUL AND WELL-KNOWN philosophical works about love is Plato's *Symposium,* written in the fourth century B.C. Plato records a dialogue between his teacher, Socrates, and six of the elite men of Athens, including poets, philosophers, politicians, and a physician. Each describes his idea about the nature and meaning of love. Socrates, as usual, has the last word.

Others described love as Eros, a god. Socrates said that Eros was neither a mortal nor an immortal, but was instead a daemon, or spirit, which mediates between mortals and the divine. Eros's father was Poros (Resources) and his mother Penia (Poverty). From his father he inherited characteristics of courage, hunting skills, and innovation. From his mother came neediness, toughness, and homelessness. Are these characteristics of love as you have experienced it?

Although the energy of love may be directed toward base aims such as accumulating money for no purpose, according to

Socrates all human beings are energized by love to desire good and beautiful things in an effort to achieve happiness. Love desires to bring forth beauty in terms of body and soul, both of which are linked to a desire for immortality. In our youth, love produces desire for beautiful bodies, resulting in conception of children and ensuring immortality for the species. The proper developmental sequence should lead maturing humans to the realization that beauty in all bodies is the same; therefore, we should love all of humanity.

The next and highest stage is the understanding that beauty of the soul is superior to physical beauty. Love of beauty in oneself leads to perfection of a virtuous soul and love of another energizes one to educate and improve the soul of the beloved one. Soul love can generate a true immortality through the creation of beautiful memories and works of art and science. Socrates gives examples of Homer's poetry and Solon's political system for Athens, the forerunner of democracy. These works of soul love have survived through the ages to benefit humanity.

Thus love is the great spirit which we depend on for our highest achievements. Love provides the energy for life's journey, beginning with physical love, progressing to soul love in search of beauty, truth, and wisdom, and crowned, if we are so fortunate, with a "glimpse of the divine."

Wow! Love is the ticket for the best seats in the house.

December 1995

Love, Political Power, and Intuition

"I'VE LEARNED TO LOVE MY ENEMIES," REPLIED WERNER Hebenstreidt, an eighty-one year-old man responding to television interview host Susan Powter. How, she wanted to know, could Mr. Hebenstreidt explain his remarkable recovery from severely disabling coronary heart disease which, ten years earlier, had left him (as he and his wife, Eva, said) an "angry cardiac cripple?" Mr. Hebenstreidt characterized his former self as being full of rage and hate, unable to read the morning newspaper without exploding in anger at world events over which he had not the slightest control.

By faithfully following the Dr. Dean Ornish Lifestyle program (a low fat vegetarian diet, regular aerobic exercise, yoga and meditation, and group psychological support), Hebenstreidt has become symptom-free and thrived. "Love your enemies?" Ms. Powter questioned. "Yes," he assured her. "First of all it drives them nuts, and secondly I don't empower them to have an effect on my heart problem." There we have two reasons for the Christian virtue of charity.

This true story is but one example of the remarkable power of love—and especially of love's political power. Even pragmatic Machiavelli advised the Prince to preserve his power by seeking love from his subjects. If love is elusive, power becomes the tool of choice. World leaders who seek peace, a natural outgrowth of the political power of love, often face danger—sometimes life-threatening danger. Jesus, Anwar Sadat, Mohandas Gandhi, and Martin Luther King, Jr., were all victims of assassination by those who felt threatened by love's power. To this list we now add Yitzhak Rabin, a former warrior turned peacemaker, who was killed by a devout member of his own religious faith. The assassin was apparently persuaded to act by an extreme interpretation of religious law.

Such is the way with laws and rules: analysis and interpretation are required. That is a principal reason why we have a judicial system and learned legal professionals. Judges often sincerely disagree about a specific case. Note how infrequently the decisions of the United States Supreme Court are unanimous.

Love is different. Not only is love not rule-based, it is capable of compelling even the most law-abiding person to *break* society's rules, to defy traditions and promises, and to create disorder and very messy situations. Look what happened to their distrustful clans when Romeo and Juliet fell in love!

Yes, love is powerful, contemptuous of conventional rules, and sometimes disruptive and threatening. Love can inspire heroic self-sacrifice and lead to tragedy. Both love and its opposite, hate, are quite capable of overriding reason. Human reason has trouble even dealing with love because love's power resists formalization in the logic of mathematics or the natural sciences. Love has no equivalent to the Pythagorean theorem or F=MA (force equals mass times acceleration). The scientific positivists, who have dominated the thinking of our time, tend to dismiss love as unreal and not worthy of serious philosophic consideration.

But our common sense and lived experiences assure us of love's reality and power. Philosopher Henri-Louis Bergson, recipient of the 1927 Nobel Prize for literature, proposed two different methods of acquiring knowledge: analysis and intuition. Scientific analysis investigates externally, he explained, reducing wholes to uniform parts which require instruments for measurement and symbols used in formulae. Intuition, on the other hand, directly experiences "living reality." We know love—we intuit it and feel it!

The inherent subjectivity of intuition tends to "soften" our knowledge of love, however. We don't rely on that kind of knowledge in our formal education, and we repress it from our daily consciousness in a society overwhelmingly influenced by money and technology. We instead rely on myths (which apply to societies) and fairy tales (which apply to individuals) to carry on the knowledge of love's power through generations. Two of the most ancient myths of Western civilization are Homer's *Iliad* and *The Odyssey*, epic poems set during war that was brought on by the love of rivals for the beautiful Helen. The power of love is also evident in the Russian fairy tale of the Firebird, in which a common hunter triumphs over the ruling czar to win the hand of the fair princess.

The Christmas season should be a celebration of the story of personified love—a love that produced miracles of happiness but also tragedies of persecution and death that resulted in a remarkable, continuing community of faith. We can all choose to incorporate the values and acts of love into our lives. True peace in Central Europe, the Middle East, and other parts of the world will come to pass only if the participants allow love to play a significant role. A choice for love, while making us personally vulnerable, opens incredible potential for benefits to ourselves and others.

May we have the wisdom and courage to give love a chance.

December 1996

Love and Giving

PHYSICIAN BURNOUT HAS BEEN AN INTEREST OF MINE for some time. Consider this intriguing question: why do polls of physicians show a major increase in professional dissatisfaction and unhappiness since the 1960s, when I first entered the practice? In those "good old days," diagnostic ability was less accurate, medical and surgical interventions were much less effective, working hours were at least as long and inconvenient, and income was substantially lower.

One important difference in physician attitudes between the 1960s and now may be understood in the context of love. I refer to the transformation of the medical practice into a strictly money-based economy from one that had always before been part monetary, part *gift.* By gift I mean something voluntarily bestowed with no expectation of compensation—in contrast to the advertising and merchandizing frenzy accompanying the Christmas exchange of objects called gifts. Advertisers talk about "free gifts" though this is, of course, a redundant term.

Before passage of Medicare and Medicaid legislation in 1965 and the corresponding growth in employment-based health insurance, physicians didn't expect to get paid for all of their services. For example, I routinely volunteered for at least one indigent clinic for adults and children with heart disease each week during the 1960s. I also knew full well that a significant percentage of my "private" patients could afford to pay only a portion of the charges. I was no martyr among physicians I knew and I made a comfortable income. Before the 1970s and '80s most physicians routinely gave a portion of their practice time to those who were both poor and in need.

The desire to give and the acts of giving are essential, though partial, characteristics of loving. Love must include a motive to benefit others, or it isn't love at all. Friendship is a type of love. Aristotle used a mother's love of her children as an analogy for love as friendship. The ideal physician-patient relationship also has characteristics of a friendship. We naturally desire to act for the good of our friends and to benefit them as we can. But the physician-patient relationship can conversely be considered a commercial contract in which money is exchanged for service, regulated by principles of justice.

American philosopher and educator Mortimer J. Adler has elucidated the distinction between love and justice. "Love consists in giving without getting in return: in giving what is not owed, what is not due the other. That's why true love is never based on a fair exchange . . . . Justice consists of paying our debts; it is obligatory—we discharge our obligations; fairness guides our relations with others. In contrast, love consists not in paying our debts, but in giving gifts; its acts are not obligatory but gratuitous." Adler asks us to imagine how different human societies would be if they were based on love rather than justice. He cites Aristotle's wise observation that "When men are friends, they have no need for justice."

There have never been and never will be societies with love as their sole operational principle. Nor can physicians earn their livelihoods by giving away all their professional services. However, nothing but social convention and personal attitudes prevent today's physicians—or, for that matter, those in other human service occupations—from giving a portion of their expertise, energy, and time to benefit others in need. In doing so one cares for and nourishes one's own soul and helps evoke the joy to be found in the true spirit of Christmas.

In summary, I propose that a proper dose of a loving attitude incorporated into our working lives is a key to keeping our inner flame burning—and to preventing burnout in our careers and our lives.

December 1997

Love and Caring

"LOVE" IS AN ENGLISH-LANGUAGE WORD THAT encompasses three ancient Greek terms: *eros* (romantic or sexual love), *philia* (friendship), and *agape* (divine love). Here I will refer primarily to friendship, which is characteristic of a mother's love for her children. Although related, love and desire are not the same. Desire is acquisitive and is satisfied by possession of the desired object. In contrast, true love necessarily seeks to benefit rather than to possess. In ethics, it is called the principle of beneficence; but here I refer to the essential altruism of love as "care."

Care, like love, has different meanings. Verb usages include "care about," "care of," and "care for." "To care about" means to be concerned with, interested in, or to judge something as valuable; it is an essential element of a loving relationship. "Care about" is also characteristic of the doctor-patient relationship. The doctor should always care about the patient, leading some to use care as a basic theory of medical ethics.

An often-quoted, succinct description of care-based medical ethics was stated in 1927 by Francis Weld Peabody: "The secret of the care of the patient is in caring for the patient." I suppose Dr. Peabody used "caring for the patient" to describe what belongs to the patient or what he or she should expect from the doctor. "Caring for" means to provide needed assistance or watchful supervision. "Caring for" may be only a contractual arrangement such as daycare for children of single parents, whereas "caring about," as noted above, is more expressive, stimulating recognition of a fellow human in need. This can evoke the necessary energy to care for the person. Therefore, I suggest that Dr. Peabody's words would be made stronger and more inclusive by adding three words: "The secret of the care of the patient is in both caring about and caring for the patient."

In the familiar Bible story of the good Samaritan (Luke 10:30-37), the priest and the Levite who passed by without offering assistance perceived with their eyes but were blind to what the Samaritan saw and cared about. He was energized to care for a suffering stranger in need.

Another example of the value of small words used with brilliant economy is the last sentence of Abraham Lincoln's 1863 Gettysburg Address. ". . . government of the people, by the people and for the people shall not perish from the earth." "Government of the people" states that government belongs to the people (the people are sovereign); "by the people" indicates that the people are self-governing; and "for the people" tells who the government serves.

Love and its quality of caring have often been dismissed as foundational theory in moral philosophy, because love falls within the spheres of emotions and will rather than the spheres of perception, knowledge, science, and pure reason. Even though love as friendship may be less emotionally based than erotic love, emotions are closely associated with all forms of love. Whether or not one characterizes love itself as an emotion, there is general agreement that both love and hate are potent inducers of passions. They are capable of generating fear or anger, happiness or despair, depending upon the success or failure of human relationships. If one acts purely from emotion, regrettable behavior may result. Spinoza described human bondage as "the impotence of men to govern or restrain the emotions . . . for man who is under their control is not his own person."

On the other hand, emotion may complement reason and promote moral behavior by sensitizing one to a need and energizing beneficent action even in the face of difficulties. In medical practice, caring about a patient with a difficult diagnosis or a behavioral problem that interferes with recovery (such as continuing to smoke after having a heart attack) may provide what it takes to persevere through fatigue, frustration, and distractions. In my view, Aristotle had it right more than two thousand years ago when he recommended utilizing both emotions and appetites with reason to produce moral virtues that are habits of right desire. Two of Aristotle's cardinal moral virtues are temperance—in which human appetites and instinctual drives are moderated by reason and experience—and courage, which seeks to balance fear, anger, and reason. He also wrote that friendship is "a virtue, or implies a virtue."

One of the best modern-day rebuttals to those who dismiss emotions, feelings, and sentiments from the realm of knowledge and meaning was written by journalist Francis P. Church, assistant to the editor of the *New York Sun.* I quote in part his famous answer to the question of eight year-old Virginia Hanlon about her friends' assertion that there was no Santa Claus.

"Virginia, your little friends are wrong . . . . They do not believe except what they see. They think that nothing can be which is not comprehensible by their little minds. All minds, Virginia, whether they are men's or children's are little . . . .

"*Yes, Virginia, there is a Santa Claus.* He exists as certainly as love and generosity and devotion exist, and you know that they abound and give to your life its highest beauty and joy. Alas! How dreary would be the world if there were no Santa Claus! It would be as dreary as if there were no Virginias. There would be no child-like faith then, no poetry, no romance to make tolerable this existence. We should have no enjoyment, except in sense and sight. The eternal light with which childhood fills the world would be extinguished . . . .

"Only faith, fancy, poetry, love, romance can push aside that curtain and view and picture the supernatural beauty and glory beyond. Is it all real? Ah, Virginia, in all this world there is nothing else real or abiding."

December 1998

The Power of Love

DURING THANKSGIVING IN CHICAGO WITH MY granddaughters, aged four and a half and one and a half, I realized again how much we adults can learn about ourselves from observing young children—children whose creative and emotional selves are less confined by history and social inhibition. One morning in a park the older granddaughter and I were pushing the younger in a swing. I heard a soft muttering whenever the older pushed the swing. Stooping closer I heard with each push: "Go away. Go away."

And why not? For three years the older had been the sole recipient of her parents' and grandparents' attention and adulation. Now she must share this bounty. The relationship of these young sisters, like so many human relationships, is one of affection and competition, sometimes subtle and at other times raucous. Fortunately these two are so lovable as to virtually demand an intensely loving atmosphere. Have you noticed how nature makes the young of each animal species irresistibly attractive at a time when they most need nurture and protection?

Not so for us grown-ups. We are slow learners about the advantage of acting out our innate altruism and compassion, tending to opt instead for competition over cooperation, for discord over peace. All of our relationships tend to be troubled: one-on-one, family, neighborhood, cities, nations, international affairs, within and between occupations, and in educational and religious institutions. Knowledge can either improve relationships or be used to gain unfair advantage.

In a commencement address at St. John's College in May 1998, William Pastille warned of potential misuse of knowledge as a weapon of power over others, creating and perpetuating strife. His solution was as follows:

"Only Love can conquer Strife. Only Love can render knowledge harmless. Only Love can transform thought and sensibility into wisdom and compassion. Only Love can bind the separate moments of existence into a whole, meaningful life. But we have become such children of Strife that we no longer understand the universal application of Love. Because Love always involves submission to deep and overpowering feeling, we scrutinize it fearfully from within the protective cage of our current conception of rationality, which is, on the whole, a heartless, soulless intellectualism. Love requires the courage to hazard sentimentality; for the harm done by sentimentality—which can, after all, be educated, broadened, and elevated—is very light compared to the harm done by fear of sentimentality—which, like all fear, is an implacable agent of Strife."

Award-winning science and medicine essayist Lewis Thomas has suggested that "We are, as a species, held together by something like affection (what the physicists might be calling a 'weak force') and by something like love (a 'strong force'), and nobody can prove I am wrong." This analogy of affection and love to two of the four fundamental forces of nature (the others are electromagnetism and gravity) equates love with the most powerful of the physical forces, the force that holds quarks together with protons and neutrons, and holds protons and neutrons together in the nucleus of the atom. As strong as this attractive force is, it is fallible. Researchers using large particle accelerators report that at high energies the strong force becomes much weaker. So it is with love—the most potent force holding people together but also a force that can be severely weakened by certain high-energy environments. And a force that when overcome can release incredible amounts of energy that can be harnessed into enlightenment (in more than one sense of the word) or cause terrible destruction.

Love is a powerful part of human nature, as seen from the viewpoint of a doting grandfather paying attention to his progeny, a humanist advising college graduates, and a wise scientist and administrator. Thus triangulated, love is sharply located as a gift to all of us, if we choose to accept it and follow directions.

Why not just do it?

December 1999

Love and Miracles

THE PHONE RANG ON THURSDAY AT ABOUT 9:00 P.M., three days before July 4, 1999. It was my thirty-nine year-old son Donald calling from his home in Charleston to share with me the beginning of what I now call a miracle. About a week earlier, while showering, Donald had detected a lump in the muscle that forms the back wall of the left axilla, or armpit. A medical examination, complete with a CT scan, revealed that it might be a hematoma (blood clot) or a benign tumor. Donald's life at that time was unusually stressful. He and his wife had two daughters, two years old and two months old. They had sold their house and had to move out by the end of June, the day before he called me. The remodeling of their new home was far behind schedule, and the kitchen didn't yet work. His cardiology practice was busy, as usual.

Because of the uncertainty about the lump, he sought a second opinion and had an MRI scan done. The tumor diagnosis seemed even more likely, and malignancy could not be excluded. He was referred to a major medical center with special expertise in this problem. He wanted his parents to go with him for support—and, of course, we agreed. Just twelve hours later, on Friday morning, he called to say his appointment was scheduled for two that afternoon and he was dashing to board a plane. My wife Carol and I went by car, arriving just minutes after his diagnosis was made by the pathologist on the basis of three needle biopsies. The tumor was indeed a malignancy that was at least high-grade, perhaps metastatic—a very serious situation. Surgery could not be scheduled until after the holiday weekend, the following Wednesday, five days later. The meaning was clear: Donald's best hope was no current metastases, and he could expect six months of chemotherapy after the surgery, followed by at least five years of waiting before a cure would be reasonably certain. The odds of cure were very poor.

Thus began an unforgettable five days. Mixed with all the terror and anxiety, those days were an extraordinary testimony of the power of familial love.

Living far away in Chicago and Washington, D.C., Donald's sister Leslie and brother Reid talked with him at length by phone daily. Donald stayed in Columbia with us, and his wife and the little girls came up from Charleston. Carol spent hours with him. They have their own stories to tell. This is mine.

I have always felt very connected with my three children. Since each is a unique person, the relationship I share with each one also varies. With Donald there are at least two special connections: the medical specialty we have in common—discussing difficult cases and rooming together at national meetings—and our irrational passion for Atlantic Coast Conference (in particular Duke) basketball. In March of this year we went to the ACC tournament together and reveled in Duke's runaway victories. Now we had cause to weep together for the first time. Philosophers and theologians speak of the tremendous power of the love bond between mothers and their children. Let me attest to the same connection between father and child under the circumstances in which we found ourselves. Parental love moves to a deeper, even primal bond. Out of this comes a clearer insight about human relationships and connectedness which transcends the small individual family group.

Last Christmas my son Reid gave me Chris Dickey's memoir describing his tumultuous relationship with his father, the late poet and novelist Jim Dickey. Near the end of the book Chris made an observation that helped him resolve some of his intense feelings toward his father. As a foreign correspondent for *Newsweek*, he covered the devastating 1990 earthquake in Iran. While helping the natives pick through the rubble for family survivors, he asked how many members of their families were lost. Unexpectedly, the answers were large—for instance 78 or 132. "Are you referring to your clan or tribe?" he asked. They didn't understand this question. Then he realized that Americans refer to family as something they *have*—like a possession. "I have a sister." "I had two grandmothers." In Old World culture, families are viewed instead as something they *belong* to. We Americans have a great surplus of having and a deficit in belonging to others. A belonging attitude changes and promotes understanding of the meaning of phrases—perhaps overused but poorly understood—like "love your neighbor" and "the brotherhood of man."

Back to my story. On the fateful day of Donald's surgery our small group gathered at the major medical center. Each spent time alone with him before he went to the operating room. Fortunately, his two-month-old daughter Ella was the calmest of all and the most reassuring about the future. About an hour later, the surgeon called us in for the results. The barely suppressed smile on his face told us the news must be good. Donald was cured! Donald was cured? Wow! That had to be repeated several times for the meaning to sink in.

The lesion was not a malignancy, or even a benign tumor. It was an unusual condition called *myositis ossificans*. Some type of unknown injury to the muscle needed repair and the muscle genes mistakenly began making bone rather than muscle. Under the microscope the young cells at the center look just like cancer cells, causing a rare false biopsy diagnosis. The joy evoked by this result was indescribable.

So, what is the meaning of this story? Was it just a very unusual mistaken biopsy diagnosis? Or was it a miracle rooted in love and support not only from family but also close in-laws and a host of friends and colleagues who supported and sometimes prayed for Donald? Personally, I call it a miracle because of the process we were forced to go through. That process taught us about human relationships and what is really important in life. If it were a miracle—and I know very little about miracles—it seems to be important that the events be shared with others. What do you think?

A Love Generator 2006

December 2000

Love Lost and Found

NOVEMBER 2000 WAS FOR ME A LOST-AND-FOUND MONTH. I suffered the loss of my only sibling, a younger sister, who died suddenly and unexpectedly. But I found a lost connection: at the forty-fifth reunion of my Duke Medical School class of 1955, I rediscovered survivors of a group with whom I lived through four arduous years in conditions of friendship and mutual support as we were closely shepherded into the medical profession. Those four years changed our lives forever.

As we looked back on that time, the stories we swapped were not about marvelous advances in medical science. Instead, we talked about the human relationships that we developed in a culture presided over by a very talented faculty. We had been as close as any family. At the head of this intellectual, professional, and moral family were our "grandfather," medical school dean Wilbert Davison, and "father," department chairman Eugene A. Stead, Jr. Both were masters of practical wisdom, as we have all learned in retrospect.

Duke in the 1950s and also today prides itself in being at the forefront of medical science. In the United States, we live in a nation and culture dominated by science and its practical application, technology. Is it any wonder, then, that two American scientists—anthropologist Helen Fisher and neuroscientist Lucy Brown—should attempt to apply current scientific methods in the search for learning more about love? The pair collaborated by using magnetic resonance imaging (MRI) to record localized brain blood flow. Imagine—at last, scientific technology with which to measure and study mysterious love!

But what does this technique explain or prove about love? What, really, does localized brain blood flow represent? Does anyone doubt that the human brain includes love as a powerful force?

A joke may help illustrate the problem. A fisherman nets a bottle with a genie trapped inside. "If you help me escape," the genie says, "I will grant you one wish." The fisherman wishes for peace in the Middle East. The genie replies, "That's too complex. Make another wish." The fisherman then asks, "Explain the power, mystery, and significance of love." After a pause, the genie says, "Hmmm. Where was that place where you wanted peace?"

Even the ancient Greeks grasped the inadequacy of scientific knowledge alone. In classical mythology, Daedalus was the prototype of the scientific genius who used logic, reason, and discovery. But he is perhaps best remembered for the shadow side effects of his inventions. When the sea god Poseidon rewarded King Minos of Crete with a beautiful bull for sacrificial purposes, Minos's wife, Parsiphae, fell in love with the bull. (Note that love overruled wisdom.) At her request Daedalus devised a wooden cow to conceal her, allowing a sexual union that produced the fierce minotaur, half beast and half man. (A cautionary tale about genetic engineering?) Daedalus built a labyrinth to contain the monster. Into the maze King Minos sent young Athenians to their deaths. When the Athenian hero Theseus slayed the monster, Daedalus helped him escape the labyrinth, though Daedalus himself was later imprisoned there, along with his son Icarus. The mythical inventor devised a brilliant escape plan by air—only to see Icarus fly too close to the sun and fall to his death.

The Daedalus myth was reenacted again in the just-concluded twentieth century, an era that began with optimism based on technological progress. Along came the monsters: Hitler, Stalin, Mao, Pol Pot, Milosevic. The monstrous concepts these leaders brought with them included amoral self-interest, sadism, tribalism, ideologies of discrimination (racism, classism, Nazism, Marxism), hate groups, tactics of humiliation and dehumanization. Millions were killed or wounded from great distances by bombs of previously unimagined power and missile delivery systems of global range.

Evil uses of science could not occur without the human ability to suppress our emotion-based moral resources: disgust, revulsion, sympathy, respect, and, most of all, love. If we hope for a turnaround in the twenty-first century, love must become an influential force in our collective and individual motivation and behavior. For love to gain momentum requires support by all of the world's great religions, cultures based on human dignity and respect, the power of individual conscience, and the innate ability of persons to care about others.

The same science that has suffered widespread abuse has, on the other hand, produced the modern communications systems that have helped make humankind a global family. We cannot afford to discover our connections within this family decades after the fact, as I did with my medical school family. That family has already lost a quarter of its members. Through the power of love, we can reach out and find something of great value before it is lost forever.

December 2001

Love, Faith, and Terrorism

SOMETIMES WE NEED A RIGHT HOOK TO THE JAW TO bring reality into focus. The diabolically successful atrocities of September 11, 2001, three months ago, were just such a blow. How should a nation that professes to desire peace with freedom, justice, and honor respond? Will reason moderate anger, fear, wounded pride, and shaken self-confidence? Will fear be used for political purposes? Is there a role for love in our response? I will attempt to answer these questions by analogy to a recent personal experience.

In May of this year a poorly understood and refractory sleep disorder caused me to sleepwalk and, one night, to fall down a full flight of stairs. Having somehow escaped death or even serious injury, I realized that the first thing I needed to do was to prevent a recurrence. I was physically and emotionally wounded and afraid. Well-meaning professional advice included barricading the stairs, locking me in the bedroom at night, or moving to a single-story home. Any of these solutions threatened my freedom and happiness.

Rather than accepting initial medical advice and limiting my life, I carefully reviewed my experiences during the prior year and discovered a previously unappreciated clue that led quickly to the basic cause of my sleep problem. Appropriate treatment has been both effective and liberating.

Using my personal experience as an analogous model, it is my belief that an open-minded and carefully reasoned approach to the terrorists' attack and its root causes might produce insights, understanding, and solutions that will reduce—maybe even eliminate—recurrences and enhance our freedom.

President Bush and his close advisors have not chosen my proposal. Instead, the President has chosen "war against terrorism" as the nation's response. This so-called war did not begin on September 11. The truth is that we were already in what seventeenth-century English philosopher Thomas Hobbes termed a "state of war." Namely, we had no reliable way to solve international disputes except by fighting with increasingly deadly weapons. Since World War II we have used the term "cold war" to distinguish this state of war from traditional, aggressive warfare. I believe that the goal of the terrorists was, and is, to turn a cold war into a hot one, pitting not only nation against nation but also religion against religion, culture against culture. The character of such an atypical war will make it very difficult to determine when there is a winner.

True peace should not be defined only as the absence of war. Peace, like war, must be given full attention, actively engaged in, and sacrificed for. Peace, like war, requires patriotism, internationalism, strength, and patience. Peace is impossible without justice and respect for human dignity based on faith and love. As Martin Luther King, Jr., said, "Hate cannot drive out hate. Only love can do that." Love and faith are not only necessary for peace but also are needed to bring out the best in people and to keep the human race together.

Can faith and love be expected to radically change those who helped plan, sponsor, and carry out the September 11 attacks?

Sadly, I do not think so. The perpetrators must be hunted down and brought to justice. Peace-loving people everywhere must appeal to the millions who apparently support or at least tolerate such criminals and who appear to hate us.

Erich Fromm—psychoanalyst, sociologist, and philosopher—wrote in his small but rewarding book titled *The Art of Loving* that love is an act of the will. Adults must learn, practice, and master it. He was referring to brotherly love, akin to the biblical "Love thy neighbor."

Fromm believed that faith gives us the ability to love. He differentiated between irrational and rational faith. Irrational faith is belief and trust in a person or idea based on submission to an irrational authority. Fundamentalist religious zealots are examples of this kind of faith. Rational faith, on the other hand, derives from one's own experiences, accurate observations, thoughts, and judgments. All of us have experienced love and can have faith in its power and desirability.

In human relationships, faith is a necessary component of true friendship. We must have faith in ourselves without being selfish. With faith in ourselves, we can have faith in others. Faith in ourselves, our children, and our fellow citizens leads to the faith that humankind can build a universal social order based on liberty, equality, justice, and love. Though such an ideal society does not yet exist, with will and energy we can pursue it, knowing we are right in doing so. We may not succeed. However, it is certain that unless we try our best this ideal has no chance of being attained.

Faith and love require courage, risk-taking, and readiness to accept disappointment and pain. The objects of our love may not reciprocate and our trust can be a setup for betrayal. But consider the alternatives: hate, violence, revenge, "an eye for an eye," abuse of power for selfish ends, isolationism, indifference, unwillingness to be accountable for our faults and blunders. Such attitudes and behaviors render brotherly love, faith, and peace futile. We must understand and accept that the essential nature of all humans is the same—a fact which is easily obscured by cultural differences.

Reinhold Niebuhr helped keep hope in faith and love alive for us: "Nothing which is true or beautiful or good makes complete sense in any immediate context of history; therefore, we must be saved by faith. Nothing we do, however virtuous, can be accomplished alone; therefore, we are saved by love."

In discovering the cause of my fall, I have been saved for a while longer. For the sake of all our children and their children, we must wage peace, a peace that is motivated in large part by faith, love, and common sense. It's the only way to end, once and for all, the cycles of violence and terrible suffering that plague our world.

December 2002

Warrior and Lover Presidents

IN OCTOBER 2002 FORMER PRESIDENT JIMMY CARTER was awarded the Nobel Peace Prize. At that same time, current President George W. Bush was vigorously campaigning for war with Iraq. Following the attack of September 11, 2001, President Bush declared war-without-end on terrorism. While it is a bit presumptuous to analyze famous people from the public record, Bush and Carter overtly reveal very interesting similarities and differences.

First, how are they alike? Before becoming President each was a governor with little or no national or international political experience. Both profess a conservative form of Christianity. Both mispronounce nuclear as nu-ce-lar. Both are stubborn in their convictions. Both appear to have messianic self-images as world saviors.

What then are their differences? Bush is a Texan. Texas was an independent republic for ten years before becoming a state in 1845. The Texas ethos features self-reliance, wide-open spaces, cowboy myths, and oil wealth. Carter is a Georgian. Georgia was one of the original thirteen states and is agriculturally based. Georgia was part of the Old South which was defeated in the Civil War and suffered years of poverty thereafter.

Bush is an Ivy Leaguer from an aristocratic family. Carter is a Naval Academy graduate and a peanut farmer.

Most importantly, Bush and Carter are psychologically different. The predominant archetype of Bush is that of the Warrior while Carter is predominantly the Lover. Depth psychologist Carl Jung conceived of archetypes to describe inborn, foundational, "hard wire" component parts of every human psyche. During early life each archetype becomes more or less developed so that the mature adult psyche is a blend in which some archetypes may dominate. The principle male archetypes are King, Warrior, Magician, and Lover. (I discussed these archetypes in my December 1991 essay, "Lovers and Warriors.")

If Bush is a Warrior, what characteristics might we expect? The Warrior is fiercely loyal to a cause, institution, or nation. He is concerned with power—its accumulation, preservation, and use. The Warrior protects boundaries and is independent, secretive, and indifferent to others. When mistreated, the Warrior seeks retribution and revenge. Force is a primary tool for dealing with others and for unifying his people against a demonized enemy.

If Carter is a Lover, how would he behave? Lover characteristics include altruism, empathy, compassion, sharing, connection with others, humility, generosity, openness, vulnerability due to weak boundaries, and indifference to personal gain. For the Lover, international relations means an active pursuit of peace. War is always a tragic last resort. Important goals are human rights and mutually advantageous partnerships with other nations.

In my conception, the ideal president would be enough of a Warrior to ensure national security and sufficiently a Lover to seek peace and world unity. Presidents also need to have some King and Magician energy. The King brings order and blessing to his people. The Magician has that special "right stuff" for dealing with unexpected crises.

At age seventy-eight, Carter admits to being a better ex-President for twenty-two years than a President for one term. Although as President he used force and built up military strength, his reputation as a Lover is secured by a quarter of a century of deeds after his term in the White House. Bush, on the other hand, has been President for slightly less than two years. I sincerely hope that his latent Lover will emerge because an unmediated Warrior contains the seeds for our obliteration.

Only love brings people together. Only love makes us feel responsible for our neighbors and strangers. Only love promotes reconciliation with former enemies. Only love favors giving over receiving. Only love recognizes the dignity and equality of all persons. Only love encourages fairness in our capitalistic economic system which we champion for the rest of the world. Only love can furnish a conscience for corporations which we treat in a legal sense as persons, absent the moral dimension of real persons.

Both love and war can fill our spiritual void with tremendous energy. But only love can save the human race.

December 2003

'Trane's Jazz and Divine Love

IN 1964 JOHN COLTRANE RECORDED A JAZZ SUITE TITLED *A Love Supreme.* The performance was by Coltrane's quartet at the time: McCoy Tyner on piano, Jimmy Garrison on bass, Elvin Jones on drums, and Coltrane on tenor saxophone. National Public Radio selected this suite as one of the one hundred most important musical compositions of the twentieth century.

Romantic love songs are commonplace. Whether in grand opera or Frank Sinatra's pop hits, love songs employ lyrics to express love. *A Love Supreme* differs in at least three ways: there were no lyrics (at least originally), the genre is jazz with much improvisation, and divine—not romantic—love is the musical objective. In his notes for the album, Coltrane ("'Trane" to his friends) reveals his spiritual awakening seven years earlier, and his specific objective in this composition: to say "Thank You, God" in his music.

He said he "received the music" about three months before the initial recording and parts were tried out in club appearances by the quartet. It was recorded in New Jersey, not far from his home where he lived with his wife and recently born son. (Coltrane was born in Hamlet, North Carolina, near the South Carolina border, and raised in High Point.) The album was released in 1965 and was nominated for two Grammys. Coltrane was named tenor saxophonist of the year by *Down Beat* magazine and elected to its Hall of Fame. He was then thirty-nine years of age. Two years later he died of cancer.

A Love Supreme has achieved gold status (over 500,000 copies sold) many times over and still today is generally stocked in stores with at least a limited jazz selection. The suite has also been part of the weekly liturgy of some churches and is the subject of a book published in 2002.

Yet this is difficult music. It is not melodic or hummable. Coltrane's modern, progressive, freestyle jazz has not been a popular item in the recording industry. Just how, then, does *A Love Supreme* communicate divine love? For that matter, how does any music communicate?

Music is a cultural universal. This observation puzzled Charles Darwin in the mid-nineteenth century. How might music contribute to evolutionary survival? Military marches certainly inspire troop cohesion and courage, love songs encourage sexual reproduction, and other tunes mark major life events such as graduations, marriages, and funerals. The best traditional Christmas music evokes and complements the Christmas spirit of love and peace. Unfortunately, commercial interests have appropriated this music to encourage shopping. In the process, we are supersaturated with Christmas music between Thanksgiving and Christmas to the point of repulsion. Were John Coltrane still alive, I strongly suspect that he would not approve.

Contemporary neuroscientists are studying the effect of music on the brain by using magnetic resonance imaging (MRI). Apparently music simultaneously activates four neural systems: hearing, emotions, motor system rhythms, and language. Some researchers claim that the human audio system is specifically attuned to frequencies and other qualities of the human voice. I have long suspected that the popularity of the saxophone among jazz musicians is due in part to that instrument's similarity to singers' vocal ranges. The four saxophone types are named for the male bass and tenor and female alto and soprano in ascending pitches.

Like Pythagorus in the sixth century B.C., John Coltrane was intrigued not only by music, but also by mathematics and spirituality. Much of this is beyond the grasp of many of us. Yet even for just an average jazz fan like me, *A Love Supreme* remains magical and mysterious in conveying its message of love of the divine and thereby all humankind.

December 2004

University as Love Object

THE OBJECT OF THE VERB "TO LOVE" OFTEN HELPS TO identify whether the meaning is strong, passionate attraction at one extreme or if it is just a synonym for "like" or "prefer" at the other extreme. An example of passionate love is: "When the young mother first made eye contact with her newborn, in an instant she dearly loved the tiny infant." Compare that usage with President George W. Bush attempting to explain and justify the Iraq war and insurgency: "We love freedom. They hate freedom." Freedom is abstract and complex in both theory and practice, making it dubious as a love object.

Recently I heard a university described as a love object. The speaker was explaining why he had moved to our city to accept a high university administrative position. First on his short list of reasons was his observation that the university was widely loved, implying deep emotional affection. Is a university a valid love object? Upon reflection, I think it can be.

Unlike freedom, a university is not an abstraction. It materially exists as a collection of people—students, teachers, administrators, and staff—and people may be lovable.

The purpose of a university is creation and dissemination of knowledge, and knowledge is one of mankind's universal needs. No matter where on earth humans are found, knowledge is essential. In today's information age, higher education is more important than ever. Helping fellow humans to acquire something that is universally needed is a loving act.

Pleasure is another universal human need. A university gives pleasure through friends, the excitement of athletic contests, and, more importantly, the pleasure of mastering new knowledge and being recognized for this accomplishment. Pleasure is lovable but must be kept in balance.

For those who are neither employed by a university nor enrolled as a student, the university still has a favorable influence on the surrounding city and state. Education is good for the neighborhood. Squabbles about buildings in the adjacent space between the university and the city or how to pay for a new baseball stadium are best regarded as lovers' spats which are inevitable in long-term close relationships.

Finally, love objects are beautiful in the eye of the beholder. Beauty is part of the fine arts and universities contribute to the visual, performing, and literary arts. The University of South Carolina's decision in 1972 to renovate and restore the historic original buildings on the central Horseshoe recreated pure architectural beauty. Add a visit to the reading room in the South Caroliniana Library and a stroll through the tree-shaded, grassy open space and the beauty is almost irresistible. It is no wonder that students don't litter in this space. We tend to be good stewards of that which we love and find beautiful.

Yes, the university can be an understandable love object—especially now, near the onset of the beloved three-week Christmas holiday. Absence makes the heart grow fonder, or so romantics say.

Afterword

THE CHRISTMAS HOLIDAY IS A MAJOR ANNUAL EVENT, experienced by virtually everyone in one way or another. Specific customs and rituals are more or less derivative from Bible stories, popular culture, and major acceleration of retail sales. They end with celebrations of the New Year. What we do "traditionally" at Christmas has gradually changed over time, influenced by Clement Moore's *Visit from St. Nicolas* (1823), Charles Dickens's *A Christmas Carol* (1845), Thomas Nast's drawings for *Harper's Weekly* in 1890, and Charles Schutz's thirty-minute video *A Charley Brown Christmas* (1965). In the latter, ever-worldly Lucy describes Christmas as a "big racket run by an Eastern syndicate." She recommends a reusable aluminum Christmas tree. It remains for Linus to recite in his compelling child's voice the Christmas story from the Gospels.

As if this weren't already a confusing mixture of Christmas customs, the right-wing American Family Association in the 2005 Christmas season led a boycott of the Target chain of stores because it perceived an anti-Christian bias. The group claimed the stores advertised with the term "Happy Holidays" instead of "Merry Christmas." (Target denies that it did this.)

This foolishness reminds me of people who claim to know the "original intent" of those who wrote the United States Constitution more than 219 years ago. If we ask what Jesus would want for Christmas, I believe it would be love and peace.

These political and religious conservatives claim to have moral and family values. What values? Some are opposed to homosexual rights and a woman's right to a safe abortion. They adamantly support for-profit corporations, the war-without-end against international terrorism, and the Iraq war. The Bush administration uses "war" to increase government secrecy and propaganda, mistreat prisoners of war, and erode civil liberties.

Former presidents Dwight Eisenhower and Jimmy Carter have warned us about fear and war. Eisenhower described the military-industrial complex which soaks up money for war/defense, leaving much less for conflict resolution, diplomacy, health, education, environmental protection, hunger relief, and poverty eradication. Carter said that war may sometimes be necessary but it is always evil.

War distorts reality by generating fear. Intermittent fear is a normal human emotion which serves to alert us to real danger. Chronic fear is unhealthy. William Faulkner warned about chronic fear in his Nobel Prize acceptance speech in 1950: "He (mankind) must teach himself that the basest of all things is to be afraid." Instead, Faulkner said, we should heed "old verities and truths of the heart . . . love and honor and pity and pride and compassion and sacrifice." These words are seldom heard from—or about—the Bush administration.

Somehow we must get beyond chronic fear. We must address more important issues than the phrasing of holiday greetings. I do not seek radical change in how we celebrate Christmas. But I do wish that individuals would use Christmas as a time to reflect on love and peace, not hate and war. If enough of us would do this we could be on our way to more sanity and happiness for all.

Merry Christmas.

Happy Holidays.

Have a healthy New Year.

About the Author

DONALD E. SAUNDERS, JR., M.D., IS A FELLOW OF THE American College of Physicians (FACP) and a Fellow of the American College of Cardiology (FACC). He practiced and taught cardiology for thirty-eight years, during which time he held national leadership positions in the American College of Cardiology and the American Heart Association. For six years he was a member of the American Board of Cardiology, which is responsible for certifying medical and surgical specialists. He received the Laureate Award of the American College of Physicians.

Dr. Saunders co-founded the University of South Carolina's Center for Bioethics and Medical Humanities and played a key role in establishing the USC School of Medicine in Columbia. The latter was the subject of his 2005 book *To Improve the Health of the People.*

His many awards include Phi Beta Kappa and the Alpha Omega Alpha national honor medical society. A well endowed visiting lectureship is named for him and a Humanities Honor Society has been established in his name.

In November 2005 he received the American Medical Association (AMA) Isaac Hayes M.D. and John Bell M.D. Award for Leadership in Medical Ethics and Professionalism.

Dr. Saunders lives in Columbia, South Carolina, with his wife, Carol. They have three children and five grandchildren.